T0273224

ROCHESTER PAPER I

THE RESISTIBLE APPEAL OF FORTRESS EUROPE

Martin Wolf

Published jointly by
the Trade Policy Unit
of the
CENTRE FOR POLICY STUDIES,
and the
AMERICAN ENTERPRISE INSTITUTE

The author

Martin Wolf is Associate Editor and chief economics leader writer of the *Financial Times*, London. He is also a member of the Council of the Royal Economic Society and a Special Professor at the Department of Economics, University of Nottingham. He was previously an economist and senior economist at the World Bank, Washington D.C. (1971 to 1981) and Director of Studies at the Trade Policy Research Centre, London (1981 to 1987). Mr Wolf was a member of the National Consumer Council between 1987 and 1993. In 1990 he was a joint winner of the Wincott Foundation senior prize for excellence in financial journalism. He also served as adviser and rapporteur to the Eminent Persons Group on World Trade in 1990 and was principal author of its report, *Meeting the World Trade Deadline: Path to a Successful Uruguay Round*. He was awarded the New Zealand 1990 Commemoration Medal for his work for the group.

ISBN 1 897969 21 X
© Centre for Policy Studies, April 1994
Centre for Policy Studies,
52 Rochester Row, London SW1P 1JU

ISBN 0-8447-3871-9
© American Enterprise Institute for Public Policy Research, April 1994
American Enterprise Institute for Public Policy Research,
1150 Seventeenth Street, N.W., Washington, D.C. 20036

The American Enterprise Institute would like to thank the Sasakawa Peace Foundation and the American Express Foundation for support for this project.

Book production by Crowley Esmonde Ltd
Printed and bound by St Edmundsbury Press Ltd,
Bury St Edmunds, Suffolk

Contents

Acknowledgements

The ideas in this pamphlet developed in the course of my work as the chief economics leader writer of the *Financial Times*. But it was only after being informed by Keith Joseph about plans to establish a trade policy unit within the Centre for Policy Studies that I envisaged writing this pamphlet. I am grateful to Lord Joseph, therefore, but also to Gerry Frost, the Centre's director, for his outstanding patience with missed deadlines. In the end, it required a sabbatical from the *Financial Times* before I could complete the task. I am grateful also to Professor Richard Layard for his offer on an office at the Centre for Economic Performance of the London School of Economics.

Intellectually, I owe much to Deepak Lal and Brian Hindley, but still more to Jagdish Bhagwati, not least for his penetrating and comprehensive comments on the first draft. But the pamphlet is dedicated to the late Jan Tumlir, erstwhile head of the research department at the Gatt. Those familiar with his writings will recognise their influence everywhere. Finally, my wife Alison is owed the thanks due to the spouse of any author who has taken an extra year to finish what he planned.

Foreword

In this erudite essay, Martin Wolf explores the techniques the European Commission and its subordinate bodies use to inhibit and distort the free movement of goods and services. It is a paradox that an entity conceived in The Treaty of Rome as a liberal force has evolved into being a protectionist one. Supra-national protectionism is not new to the theatre of politics. Imperial Preference was the same illusion based on a different geography.

Mr Wolf is Chief Economics Leader Writer for the *Financial Times* so we are grateful to him for diverting from his daily demands to take time to explain the manner in which the European Union is wandering far from the ideals of liberal open markets.

It is important to register that, if you include the Eastern European nations the 12 members of the Union only account for a minority of population and of space in Europe, though they are undeniably dominant in wealth.

Much the greatest part of the European Union's budget is expended in rigging the market in foodstuffs. This is not merely a cruel waste of resources but a policy perfectly refined to humiliate those nations which could otherwise sell us their goods.

As Mr Wolf points out there is a provincialism about the European Union's policy horizon. The tigers of Pacific Asia are where capitalism is most dynamic. They display none of the qualities of M. Delors' protectionist vision.

Free Trade, it seems to me, bestows a triple blessing. It allows the escape from poverty. Every person of sensibility want to see the poor of the world allowed to participate in wealth. Trade does this a thousand times better than aid.

It widens the choice of consumers. It is not just that prices fall. A range of diversity of goods emerges that no closed economy can match.

It is the great stimulant to management. Protection is a licence to snooze. Markets are a discovery procedure that work better the more data they have to digest. Price is the language that allows people who can never know anything of individuals on the other side of the world to co-ordinate their affairs.

Martin Wolf opens by quoting Richard Cobden. Let me close with a quote from his colleague John Bright: 'Trade has a chivalry of its own: a chivalry whose stars are radiant with the more benign lustre of justice, happiness, and religion. Trade can be scorned for no longer, it has burst forth with the splendour of heaven-made genius.'

Freedom of trade is not a matter of banal balance sheets. It is the miracle that allows all of mankind to ennoble itself.

As a member of the Board of the Centre for Policy Studies I am very pleased that this monograph – the first from the Centre's new Trade Policy Unit – should be published jointly with the American Enterprise Institute. Our co-publisher justifiably enjoys a high reputation for having done much to explain the benefits of unfettered trade and the workings of the market order.

Keith Joseph,
London,
February, 1994

1

Opportunities in a New World

'It has been through the peaceful victories of mercantile traffic, and not by the force of arms, that modern states have yielded to the supremacy of more successful nations.' – Richard Cobden (1903/1969, p.79)

The termination of the ideological conflicts of the years since the Bolshevik Revolution offers what may turn out to be a unique opportunity to develop a prosperous and liberal global economy. The 'European Union', by virtue of its size alone, is called upon to play a central role in securing this opportunity, both in its own interests and in those of the wider world.

The question is whether the European Union is equipped to play that role. Its historic approach to international trade has been an uneasy compromise between liberalism and protection which might be called 'managed liberalism'. It is questionable whether that compromise can be sustained under the pressures of increased global competition. The more desirable outcome would be for the Union to choose liberalism *tout court*. Unfortunately, however, it confronts an important obstacle to that choice: the Maastricht Treaty. That document risks turning Europe, already suffering from self-inflicted economic wounds, into an economically timorous, over-centralised, high-cost region within a rapidly changing world economy.

TRADE POLICY AFTER THE COLD WAR

The opportunity that has appeared is to create and sustain a global economy based on the most powerful – and, it appears, most counter-intuitive – proposition of classical economics. This idea is that the wealth of nations is best founded on peaceful commerce, not plunder, on co-operation, not conflict, on trade, not empire. It is

7

that States need not *lebensraum*, but internal economic dynamism complemented by peaceful international exchange.[1]

This was the ideal that motivated Richard Cobden, leader of the Anti-Corn Law League in his struggle for free trade in early nineteenth-century Britain. It was also the ideal that drove the progenitors of the post-war liberal economic system to establish the International Monetary Fund and, more important, what became the General Agreement on Tariffs and Trade (Gatt). It was the principle on which the post-war prosperity of the market economies was built. Their economic success then won the battle with the autarkic economies of Soviet communism.

The completion of the Uruguay Round of multilateral trade negotiations of the Gatt in December 1993 was an important step towards making this idea the basis of a global economic system. It appears to commit the great economic powers – the United States, the European Union and Japan – to the path of co-operation, even in the absence of the strategic glue provided for more than forty years by the Cold War. But the Uruguay Round agreement, even if ratified, is not the final word. Atavistic mercantilism, the delusions of narrow economic nationalism and the protectionism induced by fears of economic failure constantly threaten the liberal international economy. The Uruguay Round is but one step. More will have to be taken.

OUTLINE OF THE PAMPHLET

The role the European Union can and should play in helping the world to take those further steps is the main topic of this pamphlet. Chapter 2 below analyses its central place in the world economy. Chapter 3 analyses 'managed liberalism', particular attention being paid to discrimination as the *leitmotiv* of the Union's trade policy.

---

1. The collapse of the Soviet Union can be contrasted with the post-war economic successes of Germany and Japan, both of which wasted their might during the Second World War in the vain effort to become what the Soviet Union already was: a centrally directed empire. Trade and internal competition succeeded where armies failed.

Chapter 4 considers the tensions between interventionist and liberal conceptions of the Union. Chapter 5 then turns to the post-Maastricht threat to a liberal external policy. Finally, Chapter 6 answers some of these arguments for protection.

2

Trading States and Empires

'Mercantilism is primarily an agent of unification. Its adversary was the medieval combination of universalism and particularism.' – Eli Heckscher (1955, p.2)

'They desired free trade with their own people, so that the customs weapon might be made effective against the foreigners.' – Eli Heckscher, discussing demands made at the 1789 Estates General in France (1955, pp.107-8)

Whether or not the opportunity to establish a global liberal economic order will be seized depends in large part on the behaviour of a few States that can be described as 'trading empires'. These are to be distinguished from the smaller trading States, which make up the great majority of the economies of the world. For the latter, the only sensible policy is to make the best of whatever opportunities there are. They cannot hope to change the world. They can merely adapt to its whims and exploit its opportunities.

Unfortunately, for much of the post-war era, almost all countries not bound into the western security system chose autarky in response to what they mistakenly perceived to be a lack of opportunity in the world economy. But a few, almost entirely in east Asia, chose to engage, not retreat. They did so largely under the influence of the United States and were richly rewarded for their temerity.

Within less than two generations, Hong Kong's economy has moved from ruin to incomes per head almost as high as those of Britain, while the Republic of Korea has jumped from the level of Sri Lanka to that of Greece. These forerunners have been followed by a host of others, now including China. Their success has made the east Asian region the most dynamic part of the world economy and their example also led to unilateral trade liberalisation by more than 60 countries during the seven years of the Uruguay Round.

The trading empires – empires by virtue both of their economic scale and of the hierarchical political order that operates within them – are in a different position.[2] They differ in two respects: first, their actions decisively affect the world within which their citizens conduct their business; second, powerful voices inside them continue to argue what few intelligent people believe elsewhere, namely, that they can be self-sufficient *and* rich.

The United States, previously protectionist and inward-looking, has become the principal trading empire of the second half of the twentieth century. It has been joined by the European Union, which has even imitated a number of the policies of the seventeenth- and eighteenth-century mercantilist states. Notable among those policies has been the creation of a quasi-imperial zone of discrimination. Meanwhile, Japan may be thought of as half empire and half trading state, though psychologically and in many respects economically too, it is more the latter than the former.[3] Should China continue on its present course, it would become another trading empire.

IMPORTANCE OF WORLD TRADE

In 1991 world merchandise trade reached $3,506bn, while world trade in commercial services was another $890bn. Together, they amount to some 20 per cent of global economic product (although the value-added embodied in trade is less than that, because of double counting). Furthermore, as Charts 1 and 2 show, the volume of world trade and particularly of world trade in manufactures has been growing faster than world product and world manufacturing output since the Second World War, over each successive economic cycle.[4]

---

2. A trading empire may be distinguished from a plunder empire. The Roman empire had aspects of both. The Mongol empire was a pure example of a plunder empire. The Soviet Union, with its massive exploitation of natural resources and use of forced labour, was the latest and, with any luck, last example of a plunder empire.
3. The pre-eminent roles of the United States and the European Union vis-à-vis even Japan are the theme of David Henderson (1993).
4. Cycles have been defined by taking trough to trough points in a semi-logarithmic time series of global output.

CHART 1 GROWTH OF WORLD OUTPUT AND WORLD EXPORTS, 1950-91 (compound annual rate)

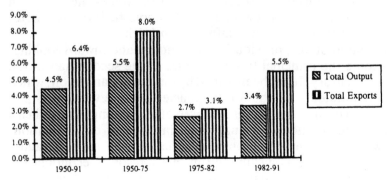

Source: Secretariat of the General Agreement on Tariffs and Trade

Trade seems to be a leading force behind economic growth. When trade grows more slowly, as it has done since the mid-1970s, so too has economic growth. Protectionism almost certainly contributed to the slow growth of both trade and income; by reducing trade it diminished growth of world output as well.

The leading role of trade seems to be even stronger for manufactures. Exports of manufactures grew 23 times between 1950 and 1991, while output rose 8 times. By 1991 manufactures accounted

CHART 2 GROWTH OF WORLD OUTPUT AND EXPORTS OF MANUFACTURES, 1950-91 (compound annual rate)

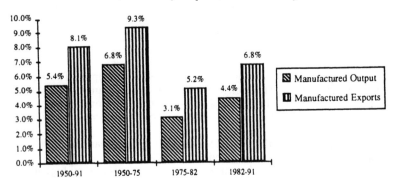

Source: Secretariat of the General Agreement on Tariffs and Trade

for 72 per cent of world merchandise trade, while agricultural commodities made up just 12 per cent and mining products another 13 per cent (see General Agreement on Tariffs and Trade, 1993a, p.2).

EUROPEAN UNION IN WORLD TRADE

By now, no fewer than 85 regional trading arrangements are in existence, 28 of which have been set up since 1992 (see General Agreement on Tariffs and Trade, 1993c). Yet the world has only two significant trade blocs, defined as zones of preferential trade. One is western Europe and the second is north America. The North American Free Trade Agreement does not create much change in the 'bloc' that existed beforehand, the United States itself. The addition of Canada, whose gross domestic product is only 9 per cent of that of the United States, and Mexico, whose GDP is only 5 per cent, will make little difference to the rest of the world. Meanwhile, Asia is not a bloc and shows little sign of becoming one.

Casual inspection of Chart 3 suggests that western Europe differs from the other two main regions of the world economy in its dependence on internal trade and corresponding independence of world trade. It is certainly remarkable that in 1991 a third of all world merchandise trade was within Europe. But this was only because trade within Europe's largest economy, the European

CHART 3 INTRA-REGIONAL AND EXTRA-REGIONAL TRADE IN WORLD TRADE, 1991 (%)

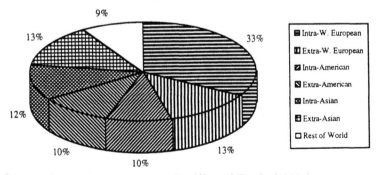

Source: General Agreement on Tariffs and Trade (1993a)

13

Union, continued to be counted as international trade, while trade within the United States and Japan were not. Once the European Union is treated as a single economy, western Europe, the Americas and Asia start to look remarkably similar.

The roles of these three regions in the world economy is shown in Table 1. The Americas and western Europe each accounted for about a third of global product in 1991 (converted at market exchange rates), while the Asian region accounted for another quarter.[5] Given its faster rates of economic growth, the Asian

TABLE 1 MAIN REGIONS AND THEIR DOMINANT ECONOMIES, 1991 (GDPs are measured at market exchange rates)[6]

Region	GDP (millions)	Shares in World GDP
Americas	$ 7,219,182	33.36%
of which, the United States	$ 5,610,800	25.93%
Asia-Pacific	$ 5,239,980	24.22%
of which, Japan	$ 3,362,282	15.54%
W. Europe	$ 7,003,848	32.37%
of which, the European Union	$ 6,089,720	28.14%
Rest of World	$ 2,176,110	10.06%
Total	$21,639,120	100.00%

Source: World Bank (1993b).

---

5. The former Soviet Union is not included in these figures.

6. It has become fashionable to measure GDPs at purchasing power parity, which increases the relative size of the service sectors of the less economically developed countries. For some purposes, this is the correct thing to do, but market exchange rate conversions are more relevant from the point of view of an analysis of an economy's importance in world trade. The fact that China, for example, generates an enormous quantity of low productivity, low paid service output is of virtually no global significance.

region should catch up with the other two in total output in the early part of the next century, how quickly they do so depending on a return to fairly rapid growth in Japan.

Each of the three main regions has one dominant economy. In the Americas, it is the United States, which generated more than a quarter of global economic product and 78 per cent of the regional product of the Americas in 1991. In Asia it is Japan, which generated 16 per cent of global product and 64 per cent of the regional product. In western Europe, it is the European Union, which generated 28 per cent of global product and 87 per cent of western Europe's regional product.

Further similarities between the three main regions emerge in Table 2. The ratio of extra-regional trade (exports plus imports) to GDP, for example, is 10.9 per cent for the Americas, 13.1 per cent

TABLE 2 IMPORTANCE OF EXTRA-REGIONAL TRADE, 1991[7]

Region	Total trade (millions)	Extra-regional trade	As % of total trade	As % of GDP
Americas	$ 1,460,000	$ 784,000	53.70%	10.86%
of which, United States	$ 929,720	$ 623,380	67.05%	11.11%
Asia-Pacific	$ 1,638,000	$ 810,000	49.45%	15.46%
of which, Japan	$ 551,270	$ 348,070	63.14%	10.35%
W. Europe	$ 3,257,000	$ 915,000	28.09%	13.06%
of which, the European Union	$ 2,821,450	$ 833,850	29.55%	13.69%
W. Europe, net of EU intra-trade	$ 1,579,900	$ 915,000	57.92%	13.06%

Source: General Agreement on Tariffs and Trade (1993a) and World Bank, (1993b).

---

7. Trade is defined as exports plus imports.

for western Europe and 15.5 per cent for the Asia-Pacific region. Closer still are the figures for the three dominant economies. It is interesting that the ratio is highest for the European Union. True, with internal trade of the European Union included, only 28 per cent of western Europe's trade is extra-regional. But once the internal trade of the European Union is netted out, the picture changes radically. Then 57.9 per cent of its trade too is extra-regional, roughly the same as for the other two regions. It follows that world trade is quite as important to the European Union as it is to other trading empires, notably the United States. It is also just as important to western Europe as to the other broad regions in the world economy.

The European Union is also the world's single most important import market. Just how important the Union is to its major trading partners is shown in Table 3. Of the exports of the rest of western Europe 63 per cent go to the Union. So do 27 per cent of the exports of the United States and 21 per cent of those from Japan. At the same time, a quarter of the imports of the Union are from the rest of western Europe, compared to the 18 per cent that comes from the United States, the Union's single most important trading partner.

TABLE 3 ROLE OF THE EUROPEAN UNION AS A MARKET, 1991

Source of exports	Share of imports of EU	Share of exports to EU as proportion of total exports
Rest of western Europe	25.31%	62.83%
United States	18.14%	26.53%
Japan	10.66%	20.89%
Rest of World	45.88%	24.51%
Total	100.00%	28.82%

Source: General Agreement on Tariffs and Trade (1993a)

ROLE OF EUROPEAN UNION

The European Union is a colossus in world trade. But it is no better able to ignore the world than are the other major economies. How, then, has it sustained its role in the world trading system?

3
Managed Liberalism

'The evidence strongly suggests that the process of European Community integration has been beneficial both to the Community itself and to its trading partners. This favourable outcome is, to a large extent, due to the fact that integration has led to substantial multilateral trade liberalisation, beyond what would have materialised without the EC.' – General Agreement on Tariffs and Trade (1993b, vol.II, p.81)

The policies of the European Union matter to the world. But the Union also depends on trade. This is why it cannot safely turn its back on the world. So far, however, it has not done so. Just as there has been a tension between liberal and more interventionist policies within the evolving common market, so there has been a tension between liberal and protectionist policies towards the rest of the world. On balance, the liberal side has been winning, as has also been true within the Union, but less decisively so in the case of trade.

TRENDS IN INDUSTRIAL COUNTRY PROTECTION

It is easy to deride the Gatt. It has achieved far less than might have been hoped. Some of its most fundamental principles – the use of the tariff as the main instrument of protection and non-discrimination – have been honoured in the breach rather than the observance. None the less, the Gatt has done enough to allow the dramatic growth in world trade shown in Charts 1 and 2 above. It has also allowed those developing countries that tried to do so to achieve growth through exports.

The history of protection in the major developed countries since the Second World War can be summarised as follows (see Stoeckel et al., 1990, p.7):

- continuously falling tariffs, from an average of 40 per cent at the end of the Second World War, to 12 per cent in the late 1960s and around 5 per cent today. The average proportionate reduction of tariffs in the Uruguay Round should be by around another 40 per cent (see General Agreement on Tariffs and Trade, 1993d, p.31 and *News of the Uruguay Round*, no.078);

TABLE 4 TRADE INDICES FOR MAJOR PRODUCT GROUPS 'AFFECTED' BY NON-TARIFF BARRIERS OF DEVELOPED COUNTRIES (1966 index expressed as per cent of imports affected by NTBs; change between 1966 and 1986 in percentage points)

	All foods		**Agricultural raw materials**		**Fuels**	
Countries	1966	1966-86 change	1966	1966-86 change	1966	1966-86 change
All countries	56	36	4	37	27	0
European Union	61*	39	3	24	11	26
Japan	73	26	0	59	33	−5
United States	32	42	14	31	92	−92
	Ores & metals		**Manufactures**		**All commodities**	
Countries	1966	1966-86 change	1966	1966-86 change	1966	1966-86 change
All countries	1	28	19	39	25	23
European Union	0	40	10	46	21	33
Japan	2	29	48	2	31	12
United States	0	16	39	32	36	9

Source: Sam Laird and Alexander Yeats (1989, pp.12-13)

* Ireland and Greece are excluded for the totals since complete information on these countries' agricultural trade barriers was not available in 1966.

- declining 'conventional' quantitative restrictions on trade (licences, import quotas, and so forth); and

- an upsurge in other non-tariff barriers, notable 'grey area' measures, such as voluntary export restraints and Gatt-legal contingent protection, such as anti-dumping and countervailing duties (see Table 4). A major part of the Uruguay Round consisted of an effort to contain the increase in such protectionism, but its fruitfulness remains highly uncertain.

What is one to make of these trends? The first conclusion is that the Gatt process has not proved strong enough to avoid replacement of declining tariffs by other, more noxious trade policy instruments. The Gatt is a disarmament treaty for people with a mercantilist view of trade policy, in which countries seek export opportunities and so trade their own protection against the protection of others. The process has encouraged both the people and policy-makers of developed countries to think this working assumption is always true. As a result, they believe that liberalisation is costly, that making concessions to countries able to offer little in return makes little sense and that cheating is desirable, if only they can get away with it.[8] Not surprisingly, the reciprocal bargaining process has, as a result, largely failed to secure liberalisation where the economic case is strongest, which is where there is the largest waste of resources, as in agriculture and, correspondingly, the largest adjustments to be made.

The second, contrary conclusion is that even though protection has been growing, it has not reversed the effects of past liberalisa-

---

8. The fact that unilateral tariff reductions are normally good in themselves, something that simple-minded mercantilists deny, does not mean that free traders should necessarily oppose the Gatt bargaining procedure. Reciprocal bargaining brings at least two benefits: first, by creating visible benefits for exporters, it brings forth a countervailing lobby against import-competing protectionists; second, by using liberalisation to buy liberalisation from others, such liberalisation is twice-blessed. For all that, the danger inherent in fighting fire with mercantilist fire is that, in the end, the blaze becomes still greater. In other words, by seeking to use mercantilist attitudes to trade in the cause of liberalisation, the hold of those ideas on the popular – and, indeed, policy-making, imagination – may be increased. See on this Jagdish N. Bhagwati (1991a).

tion on the growth of world trade, at least so far.[9] Being partial and piecemeal, possibly it never will. In other words, the new forms of protection, such as voluntary export restraints, though distorting, damaging and discriminatory, have proved permeable (see Baldwin, 1982, and Bhagwati, 1988). With completion of the Uruguay Round, the Gatt's eighth round of multilateral trade negotiations, they are likely to remain so, provided that the agreement is ratified, as seems probable.

EUROPEAN UNION'S APPROACH TO TRADE POLICY[10]

Where do the policies of the European Union fit into the overall trends? The Union is an attempt to integrate what were originally six fairly divergent, now 12 far more divergent, perhaps soon more than 20 still more divergent sovereign democracies. These countries differ in history, language, culture, economic structures and resources, systems and capacities of government, and, not least, in attitudes to economic policy. They differ too in their objectives for the Union. Such features help explain how it behaves.

Permanent negotiation. All EC policy is the outcome of complex and frequently difficult internal negotiations. Despite the increased use

---

9. This conclusion is challenged in a recent article by P. J. N. Sinclair (1993) of Oxford University. But his argument that there has been a decisive break in the trend towards greater openness of major market economies is questionable. True, the ratio of exports to gross domestic product has fallen in a number of major industrial countries, but the main explanation seems to be a decline in the relative price of exports. Accordingly, the growth of export volume looks quite different if the value of exports is deflated by a general price deflator, as Mr Sinclair does, in place of a deflator for the unit value of exports. But, on this methodology, the growth of the computer industry would also look far less than it really has been. Despite these doubts, the article does raise worrying questions about the possible significance of recent protectionism.
10. For an explanation of the administrative structure of trade policy formation and implementation of the European Union – including the roles of the council of ministers, the '113 committee' of trade officials, the Commission, the European parliament and the European court of justice see National Consumer Council (1993) chapter 3, especially section 3.2.

of qualified majority voting in the Single European Act, the aim is to achieve consensus. The results tend to include long delays, log-rolling among interest groups, policy-making on the basis of the lowest common denominator and, so far as the outside world is concerned, inflexibility. The laborious process of the recent negotiation on a common policy towards imports of bananas is a good example of these tendencies. For the outside world, an excellent example of the combination of delay with inflexibility was the tardy emergence of the EC's negotiating position on agriculture within the Uruguay Round and the subsequent difficulties in reaching the so-called 'Blair House' agreement with the United States in 1992 and then gaining acceptance of that agreement within the European Union.

Reliance on administrative mechanisms. The Commission is an administrative mechanism. The committees charged with policy-making consist largely of national officials, while national parliaments are almost entirely excluded from policy-making. It is not surprising, therefore, that discretionary administrative mechanisms are a central feature of EC policy-making.

Attention to 'sensitive' industries. Almost any industry is sensitive in at least one country. Important, in this context, is the ability of major firms to dominate policy debate in the Brussels bureaucracy. The inevitable result of log-rolling is that such sensitivities are reflected in policy. There are cases where the policy of the most protectionist countries are liberalised, but the trade policy of liberal countries also often becomes more restrictive. This usually happens where separate policies are turned into common policies, examples being steel in the early 1950s, agriculture in the 1960s, textiles and clothing in the 1970s and, arguably, automobiles in the early 1990s.

Foreign relations. Lacking any other instruments, trade policy is the central element in – and principal instrument of – the European Union's foreign relations. Particularly important is the role of trade policy in the Union's relations with the United States. But trade policy is also the most important tool of the Union's relations with all its neighbours.

Mercantilism. Mercantilism is not just a label for an undue emphasis on export promotion. It is a technique of political integration, one that emphasises the contrast between internal liberalisation and protection at the border. That distinction is clearly indicated by the contrast between the orthodox free market economics of the Cecchini report on the single European market and the almost total absence of such analysis in its external trade policy. This is not surprising: mercantilists tend to believe the domain of free economic activity and the domain of power should be coterminous. Mercantilists believe trade should be 'fair'. When in charge of large economic entities, such as the United States or European Community, they also often think trade is relatively unimportant.

ADDICTION TO DISCRIMINATION

Finally, there is *discrimination*, which is where the European Union has most diverged from the United States, with whose trade policies its own are in other respects quite similar. Discrimination is not a marginal feature of the European Union's commercial policy. It is the prime instrument for achieving European integration; it reflects the trade policy preferences of some member countries, notably France; and it is also a convenient way of achieving foreign policy objectives.

If the United States has a single defining characteristic, it is moralism. Americans readily convince themselves that they are the righteous in an ungodly world. 'Fairness' is, almost inevitably, the lodestar of its trade policies. Pursuit of that objective can be seen in the importance attached to 'reciprocity', as well as to action against both subsidised and dumped imports.[11] All these are elements brought into the world trading system at American behest. As pressures to adjust have become more powerful and more painful, so has pursuit of fairness by the United States become more unilateral and aggressive.

---

11. In a conversation some years ago with a particularly distinguished former US Trade Representative, the author was given to understand that dumping should be viewed as a semi-criminal activity, akin to stealing.

Europeans do not display a similar crusading zeal. They are more realistic about others and even somewhat more realistic about themselves. One American ideal, in particular, they have never shared. The United States insisted that non-discrimination should be the foundation stone of the Gatt. This ideal of equal treatment of all nations was spurned by Europeans from the beginning. The Union of today is not only a huge trading bloc, it has also spread discrimination world-wide.

The position of the European Union was well expressed in its submission to the Gatt's 1991 review of its trade policies:

'The Community's basic attitude in favour of the multilateral trade system has, of course, since the inception of the Gatt, existed hand-in-hand with its enthusiastic support for and active involvement in free trade arrangements of a regional charac- ter. . . . For the Community there is indeed no contradiction between these two positions. We have always believed that regional trade arrangements complement the multilateral sys- tem and represent an intermediate step towards the ideal of trade that is free of all customs duties and import restrictions among all nations. Progress on a more limited, regional basis among countries with homogeneous economies and with close links in the geographical sense, may be the best achievable in the medium term (General Agreement on Tariffs and Trade, 1991, p.16).

This position would seem relatively harmless. Unfortunately, the European Union has gone rather further than just create a regional free trade area. It has created, instead, the complex pyramid of carefully controlled and delimited preferences displayed in Chart 4 (overleaf).

A central question is how distorting these discriminatory policies of the European Union actually are. At first sight, they would seem to be very distorting indeed. Among the Gatt contracting parties, the European Union has only five suppliers whose exports face the so-called 'most-favoured nation' tariff (MFN): the United States, Japan, Canada, Australia and New Zealand. Most countries face lower tariffs, although many of these also face other barriers (often themselves discriminatory) that can be considerably steeper than tariffs. The European Union has, in short, overturned the concept of the MFN tariff. In principle, this tariff is accorded to a country's most favoured suppliers. In principle, too, this tariff should be applied to all the Gatt contracting parties equally, in accordance with Article 1 of the agreement. In the case of the European Union, however, the MFN tariff might be better called the 'least-favoured tariff', the one accorded to the tiny handful of countries not entitled to a degree of preferential treatment.

The European Union, which is the world's largest trading entity, would, therefore, seem to have destroyed the Gatt's fundamental

CHART 4 PYRAMID OF EC PREFERENCES FOR TRADE IN MANUFACTURES[12]

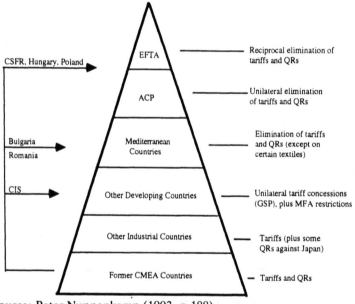

Source: Peter Nunnenkamp (1993, p.188)

12. Note the following abbreviations: ACP – group of African, Caribbean and Pacific countries under the Lomé Convention; CIS – Commonwealth of Independent States, i.e. most of the former republics of the Soviet Union; CMEA – members of the former communist Council of Mutual Economic Assistance; CSFR – the former Czechoslovakia; GSP – the generalised system of preferences; MFA – the multi-fibre agreement, which regulates imports of textiles and clothing from developing countries; QRs – quantitative restrictions.

principle of equal treatment. Things are not quite that dire, however. Chart 5 shows that 60 per cent of the Union's imports are accorded MFN treatment, partly because of the economic weight of the United States and Japan and partly because of tight limits on the coverage of the Union's preferential trading schemes. 'While total imports from developing countries other than the Lomé countries accounted for close to 30 per cent of the Union's imports, only 6 per cent of the shipments in 1991 are estimated to have qualified for preferences under the Generalised System of Preferences.'[13] This is a good example of Professor Alan Winters' term, 'managed liberalism': carefully modulated access to the markets of the European Union, even when supposedly preferential.[14]

To be set against this relatively benign conclusion is the fact that three of the five – Australia, Canada and New Zealand – are in large

CHART 5 TREATMENT OF IMPORTS OF THE EUROPEAN UNION, 1991

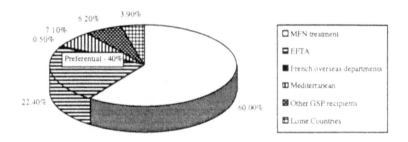

Source: General Agreement on Tariffs and Trade (1993b, vol.I chart II.2)

---

13. See General Agreement on Tariffs and Trade (1993b, vol.I, p.35). The Generalised System of Preferences (GSP) is a system of unilateral preferences supposedly accorded to all developing countries by the industrial countries.
14. L. Alan Winters (1993, p.123) uses the term 'managed liberalisation' of the European Community's preferences and also of enlargement. 'Managed liberalisation,' he argues, 'is a substitute for genuine liberalisation, but a poor one because it typically attenuates competition in precisely those sectors which are most in need of improved efficiency.' Professor Winters' description has much wider application. It is, indeed, a good description of Community trade policy as a whole.

part exporters of raw materials to Europe. Temperate agricultural imports from Australia and New Zealand are kept out by the variable levies of the common agricultural policy, while mineral imports face negligible tariffs, in any case. Meanwhile, a significant share of imports from Japan come under discriminatory arrangements, principally voluntary export restraints (important for vehicle imports) and anti-dumping duties (important for electronics). It can be argued that there is only one country, the United States, for which the MFN tariff is indeed the basis of trade relations with the European Union.

The European Union has, in effect, been creating a trading empire on seventeenth- and eighteenth-century lines, with carefully delimited trade preferences being used to cement relations, influence the policies of weaker foreign countries and obtain a favourable position for European firms. Meanwhile, the principal role of the Gatt, from the Union's point of view, has been not so much to create a global system of equal treatment, as to manage trade relations with the other great economic power, the United States.

The European Union's assault on the MFN principle, which has been consistent and determined has also, in the end, been successful. Defeated on customs unions and free trade areas, defeated too on the GSP and the Union's preferential trade arrangements, the United States has decided that what it could not beat it should join. In the early 1980s the United States offered the EC the most sincere form of flattery, by embracing the notion of free trade agreements.

Whatever the effects of the European Union's discriminatory approach to trade policy on the trading system, what have been the effects on trade and economic efficiency? From Chart 6 it appears that the main effects of discrimination have been on trade within the Union itself, which is what might be expected. Between 1958 and 1990 the share of the twelve members of the European Union in one another's imports rose from 35 to 59 per cent. The members of the European Free Trade Association maintained their share in the markets of the Union. Meanwhile, the shares of most other groups of countries fell, although that of other industrial countries ceased to fall after 1975, while those of the eastern European and Mediterranean countries fell relatively little and, in both cases, only after 1985. Interestingly, the steepest decline was that of ACP countries, even though they were recipients of some of the Union's most generous preferences.

CHART 6 CHANGING SOURCES OF THE IMPORTS OF THE
EUROPEAN UNION (per cent)

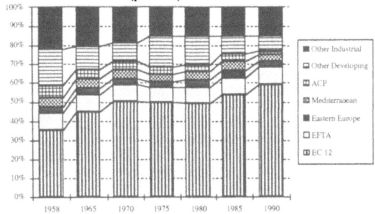

Source: General Agreement on Tariffs and Trade (1993b, vol.II, table A2)

The Union has indeed favoured internal trade. It seems also to
have favoured imports from EFTA vis-à-vis other sources. Nevertheless, most analysts have concluded that this shift towards trade within
western Europe has occurred far more because of trade creation,
than on account of diversion, except in the crucial case of agriculture. (See, for example, André Sapir, 1992.) In other words,
increased internal trade within western Europe has reflected economically efficient displacement of domestic production more than
it has reflected inefficient displacement of imports from outside the
region. The principal reason for this benign outcome is that discriminatory integration has for the most part gone hand in hand with
external liberalisation. So even though the discriminatory external
policies of the Union have done so much to undermine the original
spirit of the Gatt, its most important feature, internal libaralisation,
has at least stimulated world-wide liberalisation. In the process, it
has introduced far more liberal external trade policies into a number
of member countries – notably, France and Italy – than they would
have adopted otherwise.

UNEASY COMPROMISE BETWEEN LIBERALISM AND PROTECTION

Thus the Dillon and Kennedy Rounds of multilateral trade negotiations within the Gatt coincided with the formation of the customs union, just as the Uruguay Round has coincided with the programme to complete the internal market. This is only in part a coincidence. The rest of the world, principally the United States, has responded to each stage of European integration with a demand for global negotiations. All of these negotiations, now even the Uruguay Round, have proved successful. If ever there was a danger of 'fortress Europe', the reaction of the United States has ensured it will not easily come to pass.

It is largely because of the European Union's active, indeed enforced, participation in multilateral trade negotiations that the potentially malign effects of its addiction to discrimination have been contained. In particular, those negotiations have left the Union with decidedly modest tariff barriers to trade in manufactures. Nevertheless, the variation in those barriers reflects no economic principles, but rather seven rounds of mercantilist bargaining on the basis of arbitrary notions of reciprocity. Worse, the Union has prohibitive barriers to imports of competitive foodstuffs; it discriminates against supposedly disruptive imports from 'low cost' producers, notably in textiles and clothing; it is obsessed, like the United States, with its bilateral deficit with Japan; and again, like the US, it is an active user of anti-dumping policies that largely ignore whether or not those low prices are predatory.[15]

This complex array of policies can be best summed up as 'managed liberalism', with roughly equal emphasis on each of the two words. The European Union is not a fortress. But its policies are the outcome of complex bargaining from which some participants would have been happy to see a fortress emerge. The result has been ramparts of variable height: highest for agriculture and other 'sensitive industries', such as steel, textiles and clothing, and footwear; higher in the direction of East Asia, while generally lower for other countries, including those granted preferences, and particularly whenever there is no deep problem of European competitiveness.

---

15. For a fuller discussion of the trade policies of the European Union, see, for example, National Consumer Council (1993, chapter 3) and General Agreement on Tariffs and Trade (1993b, vol.I passim).

4
Europe under the Maastricht Treaty

'Can we [west Europeans] *take it for granted that we will remain sufficient leaders in a sufficient number of sectors to survive – in the face of countries with populations infinitely larger than ours and with levels of social protection infinitely smaller? I say we should leave this to the market, but only up to a certain point. What is the market? It is the law of the jungle, the law of nature. And what is civilisation? It is the struggle against nature.'* – Edouard Balladur, prime minister of France (Financial Times, 1993b).

'It is mockery to use 'federalism' or 'federal union' in descriptive reference to the United States of 1990, which is, of course, simply a very large nation-state.' – James Buchanan (1990, p.5).[16]

The year 1993 witnessed the arrival on the world scene of a new entity, the European Union. The name could have been coined by George Orwell: 'European Union' may be what the European Community is called, but a European disunion is what it is. The difficulties in securing ratification of the Maastricht Treaty, the currency turmoil of 1993, ending in virtual dissolution of the exchange rate mechanism of the European Monetary System, the failures of policy towards Bosnia and French blackmail over acceptance of agreement in the Uruguay Round of multilateral trade negotiations of the Gatt mock the pretension of the new name.

For all its current difficulties, the European Union – residuary legatee of Europe's civilisations and the world's most important trading entity – has a global role to play. If it is to play it successfully, Europe will have to turn its back on some of the choices made in the Maastricht Treaty. That treaty was based on the premise that Europe should become – if not at once, then in due course – a single state, a 'United States of Europe'. This goal is neither realistic nor

---

16. Professor Buchanan won the Nobel memorial prize in economics for his seminal contributions to the analysis of public choice.

desirable. It is not realistic because Europe lacks the common political process needed to legitimise the exercise of power within a single state. It is not desirable, because the attempt to bury old European enmities within a new state, even if successful, risks substituting new conflicts with the rest of the world for old ones within Europe.

LIBERALISM VERSUS INTERVENTIONISM

The European Union of today was born out of a compromise already evident in the Treaty of Rome between two distinct responses to the disasters brought about by the narrow ambitions of European nation states. One response was to dilute the crystals of nationalism in the water of liberalism. The other was to place them within a new political container.

As Holger Schmieding (1993, p.12) of the Kiel Institute of World Economics argues in a powerful critique of the Maastricht Treaty, 'the *liberal position* holds that economic integration entails the removal of impediments to voluntary and hence mutually beneficent transactions between individuals who happen to live on different sides of a border. . . . Economic integration in the liberal sense reduces the role of the state and promotes international competition between diverse institutional arrangements.' By contrast, he argues (1993, p.12), the *authoritarian position* 'is based on the premise that international competition produces desirable results only if it is not "distorted" by differences in the legal, institutional and social framework between the countries (in contemporary terminology, "playing fields" ought to be "level").'

The significance of this contrast has been previously explored in a neglected essay (1983) by the late Jan Tumlir, erstwhile director of economic research and analysis at the Gatt secretariat. The liberal aspects he described as the 'strong conception' of European integration. Those elements are, first, freedom of movement for goods, services, labour and capital, undistorted competition and non-discrimination; second, the entrenchment of those freedoms in constitutional documents, the Treaty of Rome and its successor, the Single European Act, which stand above national law and are elaborated and interpreted by three central bodies – Commission,

Court and Council; third, the creation of private rights which national courts must enforce against their own governments. As Dr Tumlir (1983, p.37) pointed out, 'formulating international commitments as directly applicable treaty provisions is the ultimate guarantee one government can give to another that it will honour the obligation.'

In short, 'the protection of the private economy from the government was the eminent idea in forming the European enterprise' (Tumlir, 1983, p.36). These 'strong' elements can be contrasted with 'weak' ones, which consist 'in the range of provisions for the co-ordination, progressive approximation and harmonisation of economic policies, culminating in the three mandated common policies (for agriculture, foreign commerce and transport)' (Tumlir, 1983, pp. 37-8). Of these, the discretionary policy that most requires central agreement in response to special interest lobbying and inter-State log-rolling is the common agricultural policy. It has also been an unrivalled source of internal and external damage. There is a danger, increased by agreements on the exercise of trade policy powers reached inside the European Union within the last few days of the Uruguay Round, that the exercise of discretion in commercial policy will go the same arbitrary way.

A contrasting and classically French perspective on the opposition between the liberal and authoritarian principles is enunciated by Edouard Balladur in the quotation at the head of this chapter. For him, as for many Frenchmen, the market represents the jungle, while the interventionist State stands for civilisation. This view is wrong. The market is a sophisticated mechanism that permits the productive integration of the efforts of billions of people throughout the globe. But its proper functioning depends on social restraint. What the State offers, by contrast, is simple coercion. At its most basic, the State is a war-machine. History shows that the State, albeit necessary, needs to be civilised. A general body of international law, binding on States, while underpinning the market, was the Treaty of Rome's 'strong' way of containing the European States. The common agricultural policy stands, by contrast, for the clumsy attempts of a cartel of States to 'civilise' markets.

From the very beginning, these two distinct concepts of the European endeavour have travelled side by side. For some, the attraction of that effort was that it imposed constraints on interventionist States in the interests of their citizens, so securing European economic integration through the spontaneous working of the market. For others, the attraction was that this was the path towards a new State. Sovereignty over the market – lost by individual member States, because they were too small – would be regained by the collectivity of European States.

With the Maastricht Treaty came a parting of the ways. It does virtually nothing to increase individual economic freedom, but much to centralise the exercise of political power. Its ruling ideas are common policy-making and harmonisation. Europe is to have a single monetary policy, a common fiscal policy, harmonised social and environmental standards, an industrial policy, greater internal transfers of income and, more controversially still, common foreign and security policies. It must also have the political procedures – greater reliance on majority voting in the council of ministers and a stronger parliament – that might make exercise of its powers feasible.

TRUE AND FALSE FEDERALISM

It is customary in European debates to designate as 'federalists' those who favour combining centralised decision-making with the reinforcement of European political organs, such as the European parliament. This description is ostensibly correct, since most of the States called federal, of which the United States is the most important example, possess similar centralising characteristics. As the Nobel prize-winning analyst of public choice, James Buchanan, has argued, however, the United States is, in fact, just a large unitary State. Since decisions on the division of powers are made by federal institutions, this was probably inevitable. But, by eliminating the very possibility of secession, the Union's victory in the Civil War made progressive enlargement of federal power irresistible.

There exists a different concept of federalism, however, one based not on the central co-ordination of power, but on competition among powers. 'The title "federalism",' argues a Canadian economist, Jean-Luc Migué, in an important recent pamphlet (1993, p.27), 'can be applied to any political structure in which the power of political authorities extends to less than the size of the economy in

32

which resource movement is free of trade barriers.' Furthermore, 'the combination of a single market with decentralised national governments can work for the general welfare, because it is based on competitive principles' (Migué, 1993, p.69). Mr Migué's idea corresponds to the late Dr Tumlir's concept of the 'strong' elements in the Treaty of Rome. Federalism then means treaty-bound competition among States at least as much as it means the creation of a superior layer of government above them.

One conclusion of Mr Migué's argument is that, in the British debate, the opponents of the Maastricht Treaty could reasonably claim to be the true federalists, while its proponents were straightforward centralisers.[17] Its opponents were federalists because, for the most part, they accepted everything entailed by membership of the European Community, including the single market and liberal external trade, but opposed the centralising and harmonising aspects of the Treaty. This is not being a 'little Englander'. It is being a 'wide-worlder'. The proponents of the Treaty might, by contrast, be condemned as 'little Europeans'.

The fundamental point for the present discussion, however, is that the centralising and harmonising European Union of the Maastricht Treaty, whether or not it proves politically workable in the long term and whether or not it deserves the label 'federalist', is likely to militate against continued openness of the European economy.

---

17. The insistence of the British Government that the Treaty refer to a European Union rather than a federal Europe demonstrates the point. A Union is a centralised State, that between Scotland and England providing a compelling example. A British federation would be more decentralised than is the Union.

5

From Maastricht Europe to Protectionism

'The European Union should use its new-found unity over trade to
push for protection against unfair foreign competition which is based
on lower wages, currency rates and environmental standards,
according to Mr Edouard Balladur, France's prime minister.'
(Financial Times, 1993b)

'I suggest we abandon the absolutism of free trade. This was the
doctrine established in our most glorious period of economic growth,
when the coolies of Asia were restricted to pulling rickshaws. These
times have passed: the coolies now sit at computer screens.' – Claude
Imbert, editor of the French publication, *Le Point* (Financial
Times, 1993a)

Why is Maastricht Europe likely to turn away even from the
'managed liberalism' of its past towards simple protectionism? This
is not, it should be stressed, an inevitable development. In some
ways Maastricht could even help keep the European Union liberal.
Transfers to poorer regions of the European economy might, for
example, limit the emergence of protectionist lobbies, as the Irish
economist, Dermot McAleese argues (1993, p.47). Nevertheless,
Maastricht Europe does risk becoming an inward-looking 'little
Europe'. The reasons are to be found in the interplay of economic
and social forces with ideology, an interplay already responsible for
overburdened European welfare states, the high-unemployment
European economy and the European Union *à la Maastricht*.

NOSTALGIA FOR LOST SOVEREIGNTY

To the extent that owners of factors of production, or consumers,
for that matter, can take either their money or themselves
elsewhere, the power of an interventionist State is attenuated.
Freedom of international exchange undermines the policy-making
autonomy of the State, which loses what interventionists call its

'sovereignty', by which they mean its power. Holders of that power, be they democratically elected or not, are enraged by the competitive forces unleashed upon them, as are many electors.

An argument advanced for a strong European State is that this would be a way to regain the 'sovereignty' lost by member States. Interventionists agree that the costs of protection by individual member States would be prohibitively high. Europe as a whole, they argue, is in a different position. With internal liberalism ensured, its economic scale would allow it to combine high levels of income for its citizens with control over their international transactions. Sovereignty lost would then be regained.

This is to repeat at the level of Europe as a whole Colbert's strategy for the political and economic development of seventeenth-century France. That strategy combined internal liberalisation, in order to increase economic efficiency, with centralised power. With its sovereignty regained, Europe could, it is argued, secure the 'interests' of its citizens within the international economy. Action would occur in several directions. Trade could be limited, at supposedly negligible cost, to what is deemed 'fair' and minimum standards – for the environment, for the treatment of labour and so forth – could be more easily upheld. European political and economic security could be enhanced by still more extensive use of discriminatory trading arrangements. The challenge of the ultra-competitive workers of east Asia could be kept at bay. Finally, economic adjustment could be kept to the rate which European society is supposedly able to absorb.

There are then three closely related sources of protectionist pressure in post-Maastricht Europe: the desire to contain policy competition; economic pressure from a changing world economy on the faltering European one; and the belief that Europe is engaged in a zero-sum competition with the rest of the world.

POLICY COMPETITION AND THE WELFARE STATE

What makes the desire to regain sovereignty particularly powerful are two related functions of modern European States: income redistribution and protective regulation. Much of the impulse to centralise the European Union comes from the desire to protect these functions against the regulatory competition unleashed by liberal trade and free movement of capital and people.

European Regulatory State
In the course of this century, the fiscal machinery of the European States, initially developed to support their ability to wage war, has been shifted to a different purpose, that of making transfers and supporting social consumption. These categories account for the greater part of European public spending, which is, as Chart 7 shows, a substantially larger share of the national income of the European than of comparably advanced States elsewhere. As a result, average tax rates are also ineluctably higher.

CHART 7 OUTLAYS OF GOVERNMENT AS A PERCENTAGE OF GDP

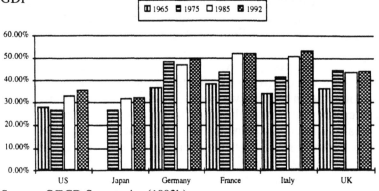

Source: OECD Secretariat (1993b)

Furthermore, a substantial portion of those high taxes are levied directly on labour, often heavily on unskilled labour. As a result, the ratio of personal income tax, plus social security contributions, to GDP is significantly higher in Europe than in the United States and Japan (see Chart 8). Among major European countries, it is relatively low in the UK, but Belgium, Denmark and the Netherlands have ratios of statutory charges to GDP even higher than Germany's. Inevitably, the burden of taxation on labour incomes has also become a focal issue in the European Union's discussions of how to improve its economic performance (see Commission of the European Communities, 1993, Chapter 9). Since most taxation falls

CHART 8 STATUTORY CHARGES ON LABOUR (Personal income tax plus social security contributions, as per cent of GDP)

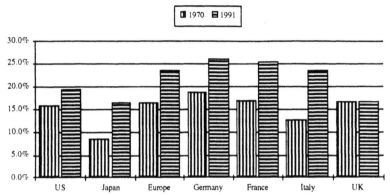

Source: OECD, cited in Commission of the European Communities (1993, Table 2, p.165)

ultimately on labour incomes, it would be wrong to place too much emphasis on the effects on labour costs of direct taxation of such incomes. Nevertheless, it is probably important that both overall taxation and the direct taxation of labour incomes are relatively high in Europe.

To this must be added the effects of concealed taxation in the form of regulations. Minimum wages, statutory holidays, maternity and paternity leave and job security are all covered by regulations. Minimum standards in these areas are to be extended by the Social Charter and, more recently, the Social Chapter of the Maastricht Treaty. If they are not redundant (which would render them pointless), all such regulations must raise the cost of hiring workers and increase the incentive to substitute capital for labour. Also important as sources of additional cost are regulations on the environment, safety, public health and so forth. Just as Europe is the world's leader in taxation and public spending, so it is the leader in these regulations as well.

Regulatory Competition

Free trade and free factor movement undermine both regulation and taxation. If a country has high taxation of alcoholic beverages for health reasons, consumers will buy where taxes are lower. If a

37

country's workers are made more expensive by taxes or regulations, producers of tradeable goods and services will, *ceteris paribus*, move where they do not bear those burdens. If particular environmentally damaging processes are ruled out by regulation, factories will be moved where they are not precluded. This is regulatory competition in action.

Regulatory competition is not so powerful that countries cannot maintain substantial differences in their regimes for taxation and regulation, even under free trade and free movement of labour and capital. Variations among the States of the United States demonstrate that possibility. To take one example: people do not, and usually cannot, move readily from one country to another in response to small differences in tax rates. Regulatory competition is merely a tendency, not an irresistible force.

Where policy divergences are vast, however, regulatory competition can become effective even when governments make extreme efforts to stop free trade and free movement of labour and capital. The East German communist regime, for example, was destroyed by regulatory competition with the West, because of its inability to imprison its people indefinitely. Similarly, the World Bank (1993b, Table 2-1) has estimated that, at the end of 1990, flight capital amounted to 80 per cent of the GDP of Sub-Saharan Africa and 31 per cent of that of Latin America and the Caribbean, despite comprehensive exchange controls.

More fundamentally, Professor E. L. Jones (1981) argued in his seminal study of the reasons for the 'European miracle' that competition among governments – diversity and decentralisation within a cultural unity – was what made Europe both unique and uniquely successful. Competition is what made it necessary for European States to serve their peoples, not, as was more usually the case in other parts of the world, the other way round.

From Regulatory Competition to Harmonisation
Those in charge of the State dislike the diminution of their power to control their subjects or to buy the votes of fellow citizens. Similarly, members of what the American economist, Mancur Olson (1982, pp.43-7), has called 'distributional coalitions', wish to defend the gains they have achieved through the exercise of 'voice' within the political system. For both sides, the solution is to spread the

taxes and regulations to other jurisdictions with which inhabitants of their own are in competition. Derogatory labels, such as 'social dumping', are used to drum up support for the cause. This natural desire to reduce competition among autonomous jurisdictions largely explains why the central organs of decentralised, federal States tend to become increasingly powerful over time.

Within the European Union, the demand to mitigate the effects of regulatory competition has already been quite successful. It is one of the main reasons why the Maastricht Treaty, which came only a few years after the Single European Act and immediately on the heels of the programme to complete the single market, has harmonisation as one of its principal themes. It is also why there has to be an increase in majority voting, to coerce recalcitrant jurisdictions.

The bargain tends to take a specific form. Countries with high taxes and high regulatory standards, which are usually also the richest, insist that poorer countries adopt similar taxes and regulatory standards. In turn, the poorer countries insist on transfers of income from the richer to compensate them for implementing regulations that would be even more damaging to them than to the rich countries which have already adopted them. Taken to an extreme, this is the political bargain that demolished the East German economy and has made it necessary to transfer 5-7 per cent of West German GDP indefinitely, in compensation. In a more diluted form, the bargain is also in the Maastricht treaty: the social chapter and high environmental standards, on the one hand, cohesion and structural funds, on the other. The European Union becomes a machine for first exacerbating regional problems and then offering expensive 'solutions' to them.

From Harmonisation to Protection
Maastricht Europe is then in part a response to regulatory competition unleashed by what Dr Tumlir called the strong elements in the European project. But the effort to harmonise cannot cease at the borders of the European Union. For outside is the wild wood. Liberal trade and free movement of capital undermine the collective regulatory efforts of European States. To this only three responses are possible. Either nothing is done; or protection and controls on capital movement are introduced; or the attempt is made to export European regulatory burdens. The last is, of course, precisely what

39

Mr Balladur proposes. Should this latter attempt prove unsuccessful, he and his ilk will certainly argue that the proper response must be protection.

In doing so, they will gain support from their past ideological success. It has now been accepted that free trade within western Europe demands at least a significant degree of prior harmonisation of standards. If that is true within Europe, how could it not be true within the still more diversified global economy? It follows logically from what has been done within western Europe that either harmonisation or protection are the right responses to unbridled competition.

ECONOMIC PRESSURES FOR PROTECTION

In their desire to reduce global competition, European governments are inevitably influenced by weaknesses of national economies on the one hand, and pressures from the world economy on the other. These are the two blades of the scissors cutting through the European Union's moderately liberal intentions.

Internal Malfunction
Free trade multiplies the costs and the visibility of policy-induced distortions. But those costs would exist even without trade. With sufficiently distorted labour markets and sufficiently uncompetitive markets for goods and services, economies will cease to function particularly well. The European economies have been showing symptoms of dysfunctional regulation for almost two decades.

Employment Performance
The most significant symptom is structural unemployment. As Chart 9 indicates, European unemployment has been rising, cycle by cycle, for 20 years. Worse, between 1960 and 1993, employment grew by almost 90 per cent in north America, by well over 40 per cent in Japan, but by a mere 10 per cent in the European Union. Worst of all perhaps, while 80 per cent of employment growth in north America over the last two decades has been in the private sector, two thirds of what little employment growth there has been in the European Union is in the public sector. EFTA countries have

40

CHART 9 STANDARDISED UNEMPLOYMENT RATES, 1973-93 (per cent of labour force)

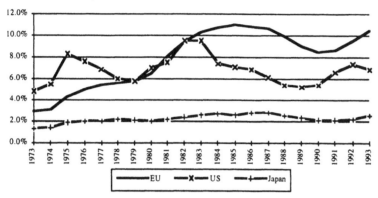

Source: OECD (1993b)

been still more dependent on the public sector for employment growth than those of the European Union. Many of these 'jobs' are not jobs at all.[18] They are just transfers by a sweeter name.

Corporate Performance
Unfortunately, poor labour market performance has not been the only symptom of economic weakness. At least as important has been corporate failure. Work on multinationals by Professor Larry Franko (1991, Table 3.5) shows that European-owned multinationals have a powerful global position in chemicals, food and beverages, pharmaceuticals and petroleum products, a reasonably strong, but stagnant, one in automobiles, a fairly weak one in electrical equipment and electronics and a pitiful one in computers and office equipment: in 1990 the 12 top European-owned firms in the last-named sector produced only 7 per cent of global output. In general, European firms do relatively well in industries where foreign direct investment is important, but relatively poorly where direct exports are important (Franko, 1991, p.65).

---

18. Data on employment growth are from a preliminary report from the OECD Secretariat on the employment problems of OECD countries published in the late spring of 1993.

41

From Poor Performance to Protectionism

The weakness of European-owned companies, notably, but not exclusively, the publicly owned and/or publicly supported 'national champions' of France and southern Europe, has already been a potent source of protectionist pressure. This is as true in service industries – such as civil aviation, telecommunications and audio-visual entertainment – as it is in manufacturing industries, such as computers, semi-conductors, consumer electronics and motor vehicles.

Even when the bulk of production in Europe is in the hands of foreign-owned multinationals, it is often weaker European-owned firms that have the influence to demand protection, particularly in Brussels (see Stopford, 1993, especially p.73). They have been able, for example, to influence the use of anti-dumping measures for their own purposes, even to subvert anti-trust policies (see Messerlin, 1990).[19] Unfortunately, protection has failed, predictably, to revive the fortunes of European-owned businesses in weaker segments of the European economy. In many cases, fragmented, uncompetitive and protected European markets are the sources of the corporate weaknesses to which protection is alleged to be the cure.

Panic over Pauper Labour

Largely policy-induced obstacles to internal economic performance are one source of protectionism; the other is a growing hysteria about developments in the world economy. The most important concerns 'pauper labour', the ability of those whom Mr Imbert, characteristically French, calls 'coolies' to compete in modern industry.[20]

---

19. There is by now a substantial literature on the costs and arbitrariness of the anti-dumping policies of the European Union. See, for example, National Consumer Council, n.d.

20. This may seem a harsh comment, but only to those who have remained unaware of the hysteria, the ignorance, the crude anti-Americanism and the racism that permeated the French debate on the Gatt during 1993. France, after all, has produced, in Maurice Allais, the only Nobel-laureate in economics who describes free trade as suicide. A superb analysis of this intellectually disreputable debate has been provided by one of the few French economists with an international reputation in this field, Patrick Messerlin (1993).

Most of the capital – physical and human – of the world is located in the industrial countries, but only about 15 per cent of the people. At the same time, technology and capital are, if not perfectly mobile, at least increasingly so. It would seem natural that in an increasingly integrated global economy, real wages and real returns on capital would converge. Economists have a name for this possibility. They call it factor price equalisation.

Under highly restrictive assumptions free trade will generate complete wage equality throughout the world. Those assumptions are not realistic. But a tendency in that direction makes sense. Suppose a country imports a commodity whose technique of production is more intensive in labour than the average for all industries in the country concerned. Then the subsequent rate of unemployment of labour will be greater than that for capital. Given the capital stock, all other industries must become more labour-intensive if the labour that has been released is to be re-employed. But this will only occur if the real wage falls relative to the return on capital. Should the real wage not fall, open unemployment will result.

This stylised picture seems consistent with what has been happening in the industrial countries over the past two decades. Apart from the sheer size of the wage gap between North and South, there are two other reasons why this tendency towards equalisation of the returns on unskilled labour may be more important than ever before: most developing countries are, for the first time, trying to exploit their comparative advantage rather than fight it, and the capacity to transfer technology, communicate with far-flung factories and transport their output to distant markets has also steadily increased.

In the United States, where real wages of the unskilled have stagnated or even fallen over the past two decades, a lively academic debate about the explanatory power of what was long thought a theoretical curiosity has grown up. Is trade with developing countries the culprit, scholars have asked? In continental Europe, where the problem has not, for the most part, been widening pay differentials but unemployment, a more popular debate has grown up around the theme of 'delocalisation' of production.

It is easy to point to the contrasts in Chart 10 and become panic-stricken. It is certainly true that labour costs per hour diverge dramatically across the globe. That is a reflection of the colossal differences in output and incomes per head between rich and poor countries. But average real wages in advanced industrial countries do not exceed equilibrium levels, nor does their structure. This is obvious for Japan, with its huge external surpluses and negligible unemployment, as well as for the United States, with its outstanding history of job creation.

Chart 10 does suggest that real wages in continental Europe may well be out of line with productivity. It is staggering, for example, that real wages in eastern Germany were higher than those in Japan and the US. Statistics from the OECD suggest that in the United States productivity per hour in manufacturing is at least a third higher than in continental Europe. Japanese productivity per hour, though lower than that of the United States, exceeds that of west Germany. This would indicate that the D-Mark was significantly overvalued in 1993 in real terms.

The overvaluation of the D-Mark has been largely the consequence of macroeconomic policy divergences, particularly in the aftermath of German unification. The irony is that another of the French arguments for global regulation (or, failing that, protection) starts from their *bête noire* of floating exchange rates. Yet it was French insistence on fixed exchange rates within Europe that spread post-unification D-Mark overvaluation throughout the exchange rate mechanism.

CHART 10 LABOUR COSTS PER HOUR, 1993

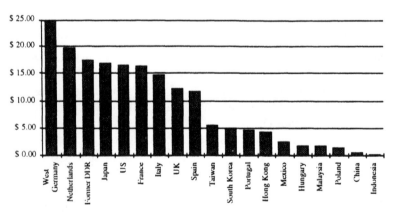

Source: DRI McGraw-Hill and Morgan Stanley Research

MAASTRICHT AND MERCANTILISM

The European Union is the product of political as well as economic ambitions. The aim is to cement the nation States of Europe together by integrating their economies and then subordinating their polities. For its proponents, the Maastricht treaty was the decisive step in the latter direction. It was to provide the political and monetary counterpart to the economic integration supposedly achieved by the single market.

Integrating Europe in this way is an historically unprecedented task. The markets and polities of the European States are divided by language, culture, historical sympathies and tastes. How are they to be united? Historically, mercantilism – the combination of internal free trade with protection at the borders – helped to overcome precisely such sorts of psychological and cultural barriers to economic integration within the nascent European national entities of the sixteenth and seventeenth centuries. Success brought more than an economic reward. As the sense of community among its citizens grew, the State itself grew more powerful, the end-product being the nineteenth-century nation State.[21]

As Eli Heckscher remarked in his classic work on mercantilism, the strategy of political and economic integration usually had (and needed) opponents. For the European nation States those opponents were the particular – feudal territories – and the universal – the Catholic church. For those trying to build the European Union of today, the particular is represented by the member States and the universal by global multilateralism. Meanwhile, trade is viewed as a war for survival, war being a most effective way both to disrupt old loyalties and cement new ones. Consequently, the protectionism beloved of mercantilists has more than narrowly economic purposes. It helps consolidate control by the State over its subjects; it reinforces feelings of mutual solidarity within the nascent State; and it facilitates intervention. Nothing would be more natural or have stronger historical precedents than for a nascent European super-

---

21. Nationalism can also aid economic development, this being one of the principal themes of Ernest Gellner's brilliant book (1983).

State to enhance integration by underplaying internal differences and emphasising external ones.

Consider, for example, the internal market for motor vehicles. For Fiat and, therefore, the Italian Government, the price of internal liberalisation is tight control on imports and investment from Japan. For the United Kingdom, however, investment by Japanese companies such as Nissan and Toyota brings more obvious rewards than does greater success for Fiat, an entirely Italian company. If the British were to feel greater identification with Italians than at present, they might accept policies that make them worse off 'in the European interest', as Californians acquiesce in policies favouring Detroit. Italian producers would then see greater benefit from internal liberalisation, which would increase their political support for economic integration. In this way, the trade diversion associated with the combination of internal liberalisation with barriers to external trade can be used simultaneously to purchase the support of those who benefit from it and be sold to those who are hurt by it.

The Gatt's Article XXIV, which governs the formation of customs unions, would seem to preclude such a strategy, by ruling out higher external trade barriers than 'the general incidence of the duties and regulations of commerce applicable in the constituent territories prior to the formation of such union'. This is true, as far as it goes, but it does not go far enough. It is possible, for example, to respond to trade-creating pressures within a customs union by using either illicit discriminatory measures, such as voluntary export restraints, or licit ones, such as anti-dumping duties, in order to curb imports from outside the union. There is at least some evidence that this is precisely what has happened in the case of the European Union.[22]

It is no accident then that Margaret Thatcher, the former British prime minister, a stout defender of 'the particular', took a liberal and anti-mercantilist position, at least where the European Community was concerned. Correspondingly, one would expect those who consider themselves federalists to emphasise the general theme

---

22 On voluntary export restraints, see Martin Wolf (1989). On anti-dumping, see Brian Hindley and Patrick Messerlin (1993).

of Community preference and its corollary, protection at the border. Such differences are also reinforced by divergent historical experience, with the French prone to translating the mercantilism that has been central to their thinking since the seventeenth century on to the plane of the Community. Similarly, the free trading tradition of the United Kingdom has never perished completely, as is true for such countries as the Netherlands, Denmark and post-war West Germany.

INTEGRATION AND PROTECTION

Maastricht Europe is the Europe of harmonisation, of regulation, of centralised political decision-making. It is also likely to become a protectionist Europe. The logic that leads to harmonisation of labour standards demands their world-wide extension. The policies that lead to poor economic performance lead to a demand for protection at the border. Above all, the process of political integration demands reinforcement of a sense that Europeans are an embattled minority in a hostile sea of impoverished humanity. If Europe is to be liberal without, it must be decentralised within.

6

Against Euro-protectionism

'By means of glasses, hotbeds and hotwalls, very good grapes can be raised in Scotland, and very good wine too can be made of them at about thirty times the expence for which at least equally good can be brought from foreign countries. Would it be a reasonable law to prohibit the importation of all foreign wines, merely to encourage the making of claret and burgundy in Scotland?' – Adam Smith
(1776/1961, book IV, chapter II, p.480)

'The state is the great fictitious entity by which everyone seeks to live at the expense of everyone else.' – Frédéric Bastiat
(1964, p.144)

'The single market will be open, but it will not be given away.' –
Jacques Delors (in David G. Mayes, 1993, p.46)

The European Union must adapt to global economic changes, not resist them. It will find this hard, for the challenges created by the rise of the peoples of Asia to the heights suggested by their numbers and their skills will be mighty. But those challenges cannot be avoided; as important, they also offer opportunities.

Those opportunities will not be realised unless ruling assumptions underlying the European Union's managed liberalism are challenged. Those are that trade is admirable, so long as costs do not differ very much; that free competition is excellent, so long as all players are subject to the same regulations and taxes; and that economic liberalism is a fine ideal, provided it is not inconvenient, particularly to politicians.

MERCANTILISM AND THE GAINS FROM TRADE

Being a collectivist doctrine, mercantilism appeals to the deep-seated tribalism of the human species. As Mr Delors indicates in the quotation at the head of the chapter, he sees the incomes of consumers as the property of the State, in the first instance, and of domestic producers, in the second. That is why he feels entitled to talk of 'giving away' the single market, as if it were his property. It is because mercantilism has such appeal that it is also a useful ideology for protectionist interests. Economists say trade pits the interests of some citizens against those of others, within a given country. Mercantilists says trade pits our nation against all others; they say, in short, that trade is a war.

Gatt Mercantilism

Because mercantilism will never perish, a disarmament treaty for mercantilists, such as the Gatt, has its proper and enduring place in the global policy firmament. If there is to be wrong-headed mercantilism – wrong-headed, because destructive even to the national interests it is supposed to promote – let it at least be a disciplined mercantilism, one subject to binding contractual agreements among nations.

The European Union must, therefore, continue to play a leading part in the multilateral trading system. Its role in the completion of the Uruguay Round shows that, in the last resort, its leaders understand this. Parts of the Commission certainly do. Its submission to the latest Gatt review (1993b, vol. II, p.83) of the trade policies of the European Union says, for example, that 'the case for broad-based economic liberalisation and for developing multilateral co-operation in the face of de facto changes brought about largely by private sector activity is overwhelming.' The Commission is saying, quite correctly, both that the operation of the market transcends the State and that it would be better for the latter if it were to recognise the fact.

Provided the United States continues to share with the European Union a similar appreciation of their joint interests, neither of these two trading empires is likely to depart dramatically from their approach to trade policy of the period since the Second World War. But the fidelity of the United States to that ideal is by now at best uncertain. The country is increasingly tempted by the alternative of a unilaterally defined mercantilism, the attempted imposition of quantitative import targets upon Japan being the most significant current example. Meanwhile, both of the two giants seem intent on developing the trading system to suppress competition, notably through upward harmonisation of labour and environmental standards and an emphasis on 'fair' trade.[23]

Gains from Unilateral Liberalisation

If a joint retreat from liberal trade is to be avoided, those making policy must be persuaded of – or at least influenced by – the underlying economics of trade. What, in the disciplined mercantilism of the Gatt, is perceived as the cost of trade is, in fact, its gain. The harder countries fight to protect what they hold to be their interests, the more damage they do to them. This is the point that Adam Smith made in his wry comment on the possibility of Scottish wine-making.

A joint study for the OECD and the World Bank of the consequences of global liberalisation of merchandise trade concluded that global income would be raised by $213bn in 1992 dollars by the partial trade liberalisation planned in the Uruguay Round (see Ian Goldin et al. 1993, p.82). These estimates are in line with those from other, similar studies. The OECD Secretariat (1993a, p.19) itself subsequently released an estimate for the gains of $274bn, while the Gatt Secretariat (1993d) has estimated them at $230bn.[24]

What is most interesting about the joint OECD-World Bank study, however, is not the overall figure, but its detail. In particular, it estimated the gains of agricultural liberalisation alone to be $190bn, more than 80 per cent of the total gain. It also estimated that the real income gain to the European Union of a multi-sectoral liberalisation package, such as that in the Uruguay Round, would be 1.4 per cent of total GDP, while to the United States it would be only 0.2 per cent.

---

23. President Clinton has indicated that harmonisation, along with global competition policy, is to be a substantial part of the post-Uruguay Round agenda of the United States. Fortunately, Sir Leon Brittan, chief negotiator of the European Union, has answered that 'moves to put environmental protection and labour standards at the top of the agenda for future world trade talks could be a pretext for protectionism.' See *Financial Times*, 18 January 1994. That he is correct is a principal argument of this chapter.
24. The OECD study differs from the earlier joint one in taking the benefits of liberalisation of non-tariff barriers into account. The Gatt estimates are based on actual rather than hypothetical offers up to that time.

The European Union does, it appears, stand to be a particularly large beneficiary of the Uruguay Round. Why should that be? The answer is that, for the first time, this round required liberalisation of trade in farm products, precisely where the Union's protection is highest, as is also true for Japan. The agricultural protection of the European Union is not an expression of its true interests. It would be better off without it.

Could anyone guess this from the debate on the Uruguay Round? The impression has been given, instead, that the principal economic benefit of the round was, in fact, its major cost. The Union has been fighting with the stamina of an elephant and the cunning of a jackal for the right to damage itself. Such is the wisdom of its managed liberalism.

The point is not restricted to agriculture. The study of international trade by the UK's National Consumer Council concludes, for example, that the cost to consumers of the voluntary export restraint on exports of Japanese cars is around £1.9bn a year, most of this being a loss to the European economy as a whole. Similarly, it estimated the consumer cost of anti-dumping measures to protect the electronics industry at about £1.3bn in 1990. Such examples can be multiplied (see National Consumer Council, 1993, pp.84, 97). So protection does not represent a case of defending the national or European interest. It represents, instead, a case of helping inefficient European producers at the expense of the community as a whole. Protection is a prime example of the delusion described by the great nineteenth-century French polemicist, Frédéric Bastiat, in the quotation at the head of this chapter.

However contrary to common sense this may be, the economic argument for trade liberalisation is largely one for unilateral liberalisation, because the principal victim is the economy that is supposedly protected.[25] For mercantilists this is an incomprehensible

---

25. Economic theory does suggest exceptions to the argument for unilateral liberalisation. A traditional argument is that for an optimal tariff, by which is meant a tariff that shifts the terms of trade in favour of the country that imposes it. More recent arguments start from the assumption of oligopolistic market structures, under which unilateral free trade can sometimes be harmful. Pioneers in this
(Continued on p.52)

statement, because they persist in thinking of trade as war. But trade is not war and unilateral liberalisation is not equivalent to unilateral disarmament. It is a way to eliminate self-imposed costs.

Import Substitution and Discrimination

The point can also be drawn from what economists call a 'general equilibrium' view of protection. Looked at from the point of view of individual sectors, protection transfers income from consumers to the government and producers. Some gain and others lose, with the losses exceeding the gains, because of the price distortions generated by protection. Looked at from the point of view of the economy as a whole, however, protection shifts resources into internationally uncompetitive import-competing industry, out of internationally competitive exporting industry. An economy whose protection is increasing would tend to have a relatively poor export performance, just as an economy with relatively high protection would tend to have smaller exports (and imports) in relation to total output than a more liberal one. This is not just a theoretical point: the exports of tiny Taiwan were $80.9bn in 1992, when India's were a mere $18.8bn.[26]

Is this point relevant to the European Union? It is, as Chart 11 shows. The European Union has been biasing its liberalisation towards internal trade and away from the rest of the world. In other words, it is pursuing what would be called an import-substitution policy if the Union were a developing country. The high domestic

---

25. *(continued from p.51)*
literature were James Brander and Barbara Spencer (see their classic article 1981). See also Paul R. Krugman (1986). Two points need to be made here: first, these arguments do not undermine the case for free trade as a policy, since the market imperfections implied by oligopoly are probably insubstantial, the information requirements for optimal protection too demanding and the probability of capture by special interests too great; and second, the recommendation of protection derives from a comparison between free trade and protection in the presence of uncorrected domestic distortions, when the best policy is to correct those domestic distortions directly.
26. The way in which protection taxes exports is explained in Kenneth W. Clements and Larry A. Sjaastad (1984).

CHART 11 INCREASE IN THE VALUE OF EXPORTS OF
MANUFACTURES, 1980-91 (per cent)

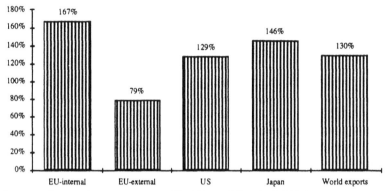

Source: General Agreement on Tariffs and Trade (1993a)

costs, adjusted for productivity, described in the previous chapter
are a classic symptom of such a policy. So is a relatively poor export
performance. Between 1980 and 1991 the value of the exports of
manufacturers from the Union to the rest of the world rose propor-
tionately not only far less than those of the United States and Japan,
but far less than intra-Union trade. Deflated by price indices the
contrasts would be starker still.

The conclusion then is not only that protection is costly to the
protecting economy, but that discriminatory liberalisation of the
kind beloved by the European Union has costs as well. The principal
cost is declining competitiveness in world markets. The Union may
do well within its *chasse gardée*. But that is not necessarily a
symptom of health. It might be a symptom of disease.

Discrimination in favour of neighbours may also be costly if it is
seen as an alternative to global liberalisation. It is politically desirable, for example, for the Union to underpin reform in eastern and
central Europe. Any such liberalisation that creates, rather than
diverts, trade is economically desirable as well. But for the European Union regional liberalisation cannot be a realistic alternative
to global liberalisation, since its immediate neighbours are too
economically small to offer more than modest opportunities. In
1991, Poland, Hungary and the then Czechoslovakia had a combined GDP equal to – and imports only 70 per cent of – Austria's. At

best, Poland might in time become another Spain. That would be an achievement, but exploiting this opportunity cannot be more than a marginal part of the Union's trade strategy.

AGAINST HARMONISATION

These arguments for liberal trade are all very well, it will be argued, but where are the gains from trade when countries compete unfairly, by exploiting their workers or destroying their environments? Is it not a necessary condition for trade to be beneficial that it be fair? Yet how can it be fair when there is 'social' and 'environmental' dumping? These views drive the harmonisation provisions of the European single market and are now to be extended to trade with the rest of the world. In that case, it is argued, standards must be agreed world-wide or, alternatively, countries must be granted the right to introduce protection against those with inadequate standards.

However persuasive they may appear, these arguments are largely mistaken. Gains from trade exist even when there are diverse standards. Indeed diverse standards are one of the sources for gains from trade.

Externalities and the Case for International Regulation
In certain cases – the elimination of dangerous products or fraudulent services from the market being obvious examples – the attempt to impose regulations is fully justified, provided they apply equally to domestic production and imports. Where there are to be no border controls, as in the single European market, minimum safety standards also need to be agreed among participating countries.

The absence of a regulation or control may also create a direct physical externality outside the jurisdiction in question. Failure to control emissions of airborne particles in the United Kingdom contaminates air breathed in western Europe. There is a case for international standards in such cases too, as is also true for emission of greenhouse gases. Yet regulation is not the only way of solving such problems. Those adversely affected could pay polluters to cease to pollute, instead. Under a different allocation of the implicit property rights in air, the polluter could be required to pay compensation to those adversely affected. The higher the compensation, the greater the incentive to reduce pollution. Either way, procedures to monitor emissions would also have to be agreed.

A kind of moral externality seemed to arise in the celebrated tuna-dolphin case between Mexico and the United States. Mexican fishermen, it was argued, caught tuna in ways that also killed dolphins. Eating such tuna supposedly causes great moral anguish to American consumers. But there are many solutions to this dilemma other than banning imports or simply forcing Mexico to adopt US regulations. The way the fish are caught might be put on labels, so allowing consumers to choose whether or not to buy 'dolphin-unsafe' tuna. Alternatively, the United States might pay Mexican fishermen to cease using nets thought likely to entrap dolphins. In principle, similar solutions could be imagined if the labour practices of exporting countries diverge from those deemed morally acceptable by some inhabitants of importing countries.

Effect of Imports on Regulations
While the above examples do provide justification for internationally agreed standards in trade, there are cases where trade among countries with diverse preferences and regulations can help everyone involved. It does so by giving them more (or less) of what they want (or do not want). Those cases principally concern the domestic regulation of 'bads'. Suppose, for example, that two countries, similar in other ways, have different preferences for, and consequently different regulations on, the emission of pollutants whose effects are felt locally. Provided barriers to trade are small, polluting processes will move to the country with the more liberal regulations. In this case, the country that has imposed the tighter regulation loses the processes its people dislikes, while still enjoying, through trade, the products they desire.

Trade works like a turbo-charger on a car: it makes the effects of regulations more dramatic than they would be without it. The aims of such regulations are secured at lower economic cost. To attempt to regulate emissions, while adopting protection to prevent the resultant flight of the polluting industry is absurd. Why, then, is this apparently benign process denigrated as environmental dumping? The reason is that loss of jobs to imports makes the implications of the regulation more visible. Such transparency is precisely what politicians wish to avoid. It is relatively easy to impose regulations whose costs fall on the public at large. It is more difficult to do so if costs fall on specific groups of workers.

Control over 'bads' is, however, only one aspect of regulation. As the great French nineteenth-century polemicist for free trade, Frédéric Bastiat, argued in the quotation at the head of the chapter, most politics are about the distribution of income. As the previous chapter showed, this is even truer today than when Bastiat was alive. If resources are to be redistributed, however, they must first be made captive. But free trade – including mobility of capital, labour and ideas – makes resources less captive. It provides those who own them with greater freedom to evade exactions imposed on behalf of those who lack them. The extent of the increased freedom – and the consequent threat to taxation and regulation – must not be exaggerated. But trade will tend to even out the extremes, as jurisdictions compete with one another for mobile resources and buyers move to places that offer the cheapest purchases. The monopoly power of the State will be eroded by trade.

Consider, for example, minimum wages, a regulation with a purely redistributive intent. High minimum wages transfer income from capital to certain workers. They also tend to increase unemployment, as capital is substituted for labour. The relative size of these effects depends on the responsiveness of employment to the cost of labour. If responsiveness is low, income redistribution will dominate increased unemployment.

The possibility of imports will make that outcome substantially less likely. Under autarky, minimum wages raise the relative cost of labour-intensive products. Under liberal trade, however, the relative prices of those products are prevented from rising. Instead, imports replace part or all of domestic production, thereby creating substantially more unemployment than under autarky. Under liberal trade it is far more difficult to tax capital in favour of labour. With free movement of capital, it becomes more difficult still.

Effects of Harmonisation on Exporters
While free trade will indeed tend to undermine redistributive regulations in importing countries and will also make the costs of regulation more transparent, its opposite, protection, will not

benefit workers in exporting countries as is sometimes argued. The low wages of such countries as India or China reflect their poverty. Raising the wages of a chosen few engaged in visible formal sector production will slow economic development and reduce the rate at which labour is absorbed into modern production. It is for this perfectly moral reason that virtually every country in the world, including the advanced industrial countries of today, suppressed or restricted trade union activities when large quantities of low productivity labour still had to be shifted into industry from agriculture – or, in the case of countries of immigration, from abroad. Similarly, even child labour may be inevitable in a country as poor as Bangladesh, for lack of any alternative, other than starvation. Again, industrial countries barred child labour only when most parents were rich enough to afford to keep their children idle throughout childhood.

If arguments for higher labour standards in the interests of citizens of poor exporting countries carry a mild stench of hypocrisy, demands for the imposition of environmental standards simply reek of it. Citizens of European countries that have eliminated all large wild animals insist that Indians must protect their tigers and Africans their elephants. Similarly, citizens of countries that have destroyed their forests demand that developing countries keep theirs standing, on pain of trade sanctions. And why should they do that? To reduce global warming, comes the answer.

Yet whose emission of greenhouse gases is it that is creating this danger? In 1989 some 60 per cent of global emissions of greenhouse gases came from the 15 per cent of the global population who live in the advanced industrial countries (see World Bank, 1992, fig.6). Furthermore, their emissions per head were almost three and a half times greater than those of people living in middle-income developing countries and ten times greater than those of people living in low-income countries, among whom fall China and India. If the rich wish the poor to behave in ways different from themselves, they should have the decency to pay them. Otherwise, both here and in the case of labour standards, the rich countries are merely proposing to punish the poor for their poverty.

Benefits of Diversity[27]

Arguments for the agreement and implementation of some international, or global, standards have force. But diversity should normally be welcomed. This is as true within Europe as it is globally.

In the first place, competition among regimes with different regulations and policies has been an important source of human advance. In particular, it provides a bolt hole for the persecuted, the oppressed or the overtaxed. The existence of such refuges can, in turn, influence the policies of oppressive governments, sometimes dramatically so.

In the second place, regulatory diversity is a natural and proper reflection of differences in incomes, natural resources and values. Inhabitants of wealthy countries will have different preferences for work and leisure, as well as for the environment, from inhabitants of poor ones.[28] Similarly, peoples with access to vast open spaces will value the environment differently from inhabitants of more densely populated countries. Again, peasants whose crops are threatened by elephants will value them differently from the children of Surrey stockbrokers.

In the third place, trade under regulatory diversity makes the effects of intervention more transparent. By making intervention more transparent, inappropriate interventions – such as minimum wages – should be rendered more difficult to impose. In addition, trade makes the regulation of 'bads' even more effective than it would otherwise be, by forcing production away from the most disliked activities.

Finally, harmonisation of regulatory regimes can readily lead to outright protection, so turning into a way of punishing the poor for their poverty. International harmonisation must, in any case, be limited to what can be agreed and enforced. The alternative to consent is coercion. But not only are there limits to its feasibility,

---

27. A discussion of the arguments for harmonisation among trading nations is contained in Jagdish N. Bhagwati (1993), part of a Ford Foundation project on the problem raised by the growing demand to remove domestic differences prior to freeing trade.
28. It is often forgotten how big international income differences are: even measured at common international prices, the incomes per head of the Swiss are twenty times higher than those of Indians (see World Bank, 1993a, table 30).

there is also a risk that coercion would undermine the legitimacy of an international regime.

PAUPER LABOUR IN PERSPECTIVE

Some protectionists – Mr Balladur seems to be one – hope that the mere act of imposing minimum labour standards on a country like China will eliminate its comparative advantage in labour-intensive products. They are wrong. Under any justifiable regulations, the price of labour in China will still be kept down, as it should be, by the negligible opportunity cost of surplus farm labour. Any minimum standards that might drive a substantial wedge between labour costs in advanced factories and the opportunity cost of labour would be both economically inefficient and certain to generate unemployment.

This then raises a worry deeper even than that about standards. It is about the effects of a flood of cheap labour-intensive exports from countries with infinite supplies of low wage labour. Two question arise: first, how significant an effect might such imports have on wages and employment in industrial countries? Second, is protection the right alternative?

The extent to which exports of manufactures have already driven down demand for – and relative wages of – unskilled labour in rich countries is controversial. Adrian Wood (1991; 1994) of the Institute of Development Studies at Sussex University, for example, argues that the cumulative effect, to 1990, of North-South trade in manufactures was to lower demand for unskilled labour in Northern economies, as a proportion of 1985 employment, by 6 per cent and demand for manufacturing labour by 12 per cent. These are not negligible figures.

Simultaneously, however, Jagdish Bhagwati (1991b) of Columbia University has called into question the conclusion reached in such studies, including those of influential labour-economists working in the United States, that imports of commodities that use unskilled labour intensively had been responsible for the decline in the real wages of unskilled labour in the United States in the 1980s. He has argued that, if this were indeed so, the relative prices of such labour-intensive imports should have fallen. But this they did not seem to have done.

Subsequently, two American academics, Robert Lawrence (1993) of Harvard University and Matthew Slaughter of the Massachusetts Institute of Technology, investigated this objection, to find that the relative prices of labour-intensive goods had not fallen and that the factor proportions within these industries had also gone in a direction opposite to what would be predicted by the hypothesis that trade with poor countries was producing paupers in the United States. They concluded that trade 'has not been the major contributor to the performance of US average and relative wages in the 1980s'.[29]

Whatever the truth about the past, continued rapid expansion of exports of manufactures from developing countries may have an effect on future demand for unskilled labour. Protection is the idiot's answer. But piecemeal protection would be irrelevant. High and sustained protection against imports of labour-intensive manufactures would be needed. Such a policy would be open to powerful objections: it would fail to preserve lost export markets, unless rich countries were to combine to create a discriminatory free trade area against poorer ones. It would shift resources from efficient export industry to inefficient import-competing industry. It would lower aggregate economic welfare, by foregoing the gains from trade, and impose a large tax on consumers of labour-intensive products in rich countries, many of them poor. It would also create growing friction between old economic powers and new ones.

A far better response would be a mixture of increased investment in education with subsidies to unskilled employment. This would require redirection of welfare state spending, with the relatively better off bearing more of the cost of their own pensions and health spending. Pressures to retreat behind a protectionist wall against Asian exporters of manufactures are bound to grow. Defeating those pressures will need courage and imagination. Morally, it would be wrong to block the peaceful commercial road to economic progress. To avoid redistributing income openly among ourselves, the hopes of hundreds of millions of people would be blighted.

---

29. This conclusion is also supported in a review article by Jagdish Bhagwati and Vivek Dehejia (1993).

Practically, the enticing economic opportunities created by the global spread of industrialisation would also be foregone.

SOVEREIGNTY AND LIBERAL TRADE

The market is cosmopolitan and individualistic; the State is national and collectivist. The reconciliation sometimes envisaged is that the market should be free only if it falls within the control of States. In the European debate this view is often represented by the thesis that member States have lost their sovereignty, but that it can be regained by pooling it within the European Union. Europe needs to be a State because its member States are no longer sovereign.

This argument is mistaken. Member States are still sovereign in two quite different meanings of that abused term. First, they remain juridically sovereign, since sovereignty refers not to power but to ultimate legal authority. Secondly, they still possess the most significant form of economic power, which is that to facilitate the prosperity of their citizens. Contrary to what the Euro-mercantilists are prone to argue, experience and theory both demonstrate that small States are just as economically sovereign in this respect as big ones. By educating their citizens, by offering efficient public administrations and by guaranteeing property rights, States as small as Singapore, the Republic of China (Taiwan), Norway, Switzerland or Sweden have achieved extraordinary economic success.

The significant difference has not been between big countries and small ones, but between those governments that provided what their citizens needed for profitable participation in the international economy and those that did not. The idea that government must be co-extensive with the market is wrong. It may even be the case that small States, knowing the limitations on the sensible exercise of power, are less likely to undertake economically damaging interventions. It is noticeable both how many of the world's richest countries are small and how many of its poor ones are very large. China and India, both impoverished giants, demonstrate the point.

The individual member States of the European Union are, in short, not too small to exercise sovereignty both effectively and beneficially. Moreover, where they are indeed unable to act, the European Union is often not the answer. The most significant environmental problems, for example, are local or global, but not European.

Europe does not, therefore, need to become a mercantilist super-State, with a capital in Brussels. Such political gigantism may perhaps be needed to secure Europe's military security. But it would be economically counterproductive. Europe's choices should, for the most part, be decentralisation and liberal trade, not harmonisation and protectionism. Common policies towards the rest of the world will be needed, but the more rule-bound and stable are the European Union's policies, the less activist the policy-making it will need.

This does not mean all harmonisation of regulations is undesirable, be it within the European Union or globally. Cases arise where the regulatory 'race to the bottom' could be damaging for all concerned. But the saliency of those cases is frequently exaggerated and the costs of inappropriate standards underestimated. Furthermore, while free trade and free factor movements do reduce the ability of individual governments to impose regulation and taxation, the responsiveness of trade and factor flows is not generally so high as to eliminate the freedom of action of governments: far from it, in fact, as the government of tiny Singapore has demonstrated. Thus, regulatory harmonisation is, for the most part, justified neither by the danger posed by free trade to essential regulations nor by the impotence of governments in the face of the market.

If the European Union makes the wrong internal choices about regulatory harmonisation, its efforts might render the European economy unable to participate effectively in the world economy, because it would have become too rigid and too lacking in dynamism. That would be a tragedy for Europe and a pity for the rest of the world. With the United States increasingly protectionist, great damage could yet be done to the liberal global economy.

If the European Union makes the wrong external choice about protection, the danger it faces is marginalisation. Despite the fact that the European Union is the world's largest trading entity, it is already excluded from discussions that may prove vital to the future of the world's economic system. The development of Asia-Pacific Economic Co-operation (APEC), which includes east Asia and north America, but excludes the Union, is disturbing. But this development has largely occurred for two reasons: first, because the

Union has pursued a discriminatory trade policy directed against many successful Asian nations and, second, because it is no longer viewed as a dynamic element in the world economy.

As new competitors continue to press on the European economy, there will be a natural inclination to pull up the drawbridge. Trade with these countries is, it will be argued, too uncomfortable and the European economy is, in any case, too large to need much external trade. Europe should organise itself, instead, on the basis of self-sufficiency. Before Europeans do decide to go down that road, they might remember a precedent.

Five hundred years ago China was the world's richest State. Proud in its sovereign independence and sure of its cultural supremacy, the imperial court made trade with barbarians illegal. Cut off from developments elsewhere, China became ever more relatively backward. Europe, like China, has no divine right to its current wealth and influence. It has to earn them. It can do so only by staying true to the twin sources of that wealth: trade and competition.

EUROPEAN UNION IN A GLOBAL CONTEXT

What will happen to the external role of the European Union? Much will depend on its internal development. But much will also depend on what happens elsewhere. If, as seems increasingly likely, the United States under president Clinton is prepared to embrace the Gatt rhetorically, while ignoring its fundamental principles, the Union will follow suit. By blaming foreigners for the alleged failure of the United States to export, the Clinton administration is playing into the hands of domestic protectionists. Too many Europeans are attracted by the notion of fortress Europe not to try to follow such a lead. The danger is that the naïve mercantilists on both sides of the Atlantic will join hands and dance to the protectionist tune, pointing in excuse to their cousins in Japan or China. If so, this will ruin virtually everything achieved over the past fifty years. The trading empires can do far better than that. In their own interests, they must.

Bibliography

Baldwin, Robert (1982) *The Inefficacy of Trade Policy*, Princeton University Essays in International Finance, no. 150, Princeton, N.J., Department of Economics, Princeton University.

Bastiat, Frédéric (1964) 'The State,' reprinted in *Selected Essays on Political Economy*, New York: The Foundation for Economic Research.

Bhagwati, Jagdish N. (1988) *Protectionism*, Cambridge, Mass: MIT Press.

Bhagwati, Jagdish N. (1991a) *The World Trading System at Risk*, New York: Harvester Wheatsheaf.

Bhagwati, Jagdish N. (1991b) *Free Traders and Free Immigrationists: Strangers or Friends?* Working Paper no. 20, New York: Russell Sage Foundation.

Bhagwati, Jagdish N. (1993) 'The Demands to Reduce Domestic Diversity among Trading Nations', mimeo, Ford Foundation.

Bhagwati, Jagdish N. and Vivek Dehejia (1993) 'Free Trade and Wages of the Unskilled: Is Marx Striking Again?', paper presented at a conference on the Influence of International Trade on U.S. wages organised by the American Enterprise Institute, 10 September.

Brander, James and Barbara Spencer (1981) 'Tariffs and the Extraction of Foreign Monopoly Rents under Potential Entry', *Canadian Journal of Economics*, vol. 14, pp.371-89.

Buchanan, James M. (1990) 'An American Perspective on Europe's Constitutional Opportunity', paper presented at the Mont Pélérin Society's general meeting on 'Europe in an Open World Economy', 2-8 September.

Clements, Kenneth W. and Larry A. Sjaastad (1984) *How Protectionism Taxes Exporters*, Thames Essay no. 39, London: Trade Policy Research Centre.

Cobden, Richard (1903) 'America', in *The Political Writings of Richard Cobden*, vol. 1, London: T. Fisher Unwin, reprinted New York: Klaus reprint, 1969.

Commission of the European Communities (1993) *Growth, Com-*

petitiveness, Employment: the Challenges and Ways forward into the 21st Century, White Paper, 5 December, COM (93) 700, Brussels.

Financial Times (1993a) 'Visions of Europe: a Pressing Case for Protection', 1 June.

Financial Times (1993b) 'Baladur calls for EU action against "unfair" trade', 31 December.

Franko, L. G. (1991) 'Global corporate competition II: Is the large American firm an endangered species?' *Business Horizons*, vol. 34, no. 6, November-December, cited in John M. Stopford, 'European multinationals' competitiveness: Implications for trade policy', in David G. Mayes (ed.) *The External Implications of European Integration*, New York: Harvester Wheatsheaf.

Gellner, Ernest (1983) *Nations and Nationalism*, Oxford: Basil Blackwell.

General Agreement on Tariffs and Trade (1991). *Trade Policy Review: the European Communities*. Report by the European Communities, C/RM/G/10, 18 March, Geneva.

General Agreement on Tariffs and Trade (1993a) *International Trade 91-92. Statistics*, Geneva.

General Agreement on Tariffs and Trade (1993b) *Trade Policy Review: European Communities*, vols I and II, Geneva.

General Agreement on Tariffs and Trade (1993c) 'Regional Trading Arrangements should be Building Blocks, not Stumbling Blocks – says Sutherland', Gatt/1596. Press Communiqué, 16 September.

General Agreement on Tariffs and Trade (1993d) Background paper on the results of the Uruguay Round for developing countries, 29 November.

General Agreement on Tariffs and Trade (1993e) *Gatt Background Paper looks at Value of Possible Round Results, especially to Developing Countries*, News of the Uruguay Round, no. 078 December.

Goldin, Ian, Odin Knudsen and Dominique van de Mensbrugghe (1993) *Trade Liberalisation: Global Economic Implications*, Paris: Organisation for Economic Co-operation and Development and the World Bank.

Heckscher, Eli (1955) *Mercantilism*, revised 2nd ed., E. F. Söderlund, trans. Mendel Shapiro, London: Bradford and Dickens.

Henderson, David (1993) 'The EC, the US and Others in a Changing World Economy', *The World Economy*, vol. 16, no. 5, September, pp.537-52.

Hindley, Brian and Patrick Messerlin (1993) 'Guarantees of Market Access and Regionalism', in Kym Anderson and Richard Blackhurst (eds) *Regional Integration and the Global Trading System*, New York: Harvester Wheatsheaf.

Jones, E. L. (1981) *The European Miracle: Environments, economics and geopolitics in history of Europe and Asia*, Cambridge: Cambridge University Press.

Krugman, Paul R. (1986) (ed.) *Strategic Trade Policy and the New International Economics*, Cambridge, Mass: MIT Press.

Laird, Sam and Alexander Yeats (1989) 'Nontariff Barriers of Developed Countries, 1966-86', *Finance and Development*, March.

Lawrence, Robert Z. and Matthew J. Slaughter (1993) 'Trade and US Wages: Great Sucking Sound or Small Hiccup?' *Brookings Papers on Economic Activity, Microeconomics*, no. 2.

McAleese, Dermot (1993) 'The Community's External Trade Policy', in David G. Mayes (ed.) *The External Implications of European Integration*, New York: Harvester Wheatsheaf.

Mayes, David G. (ed.) (1993) *The External Implications of European Integration*, New York: Harvester Wheatsheaf.

Messerlin, Patrick A. (1990) 'Anti-Dumping Regulations or Pro-Cartel Law? The EC Chemical Cases', *The World Economy*, vol. 13, no. 4, December.

Messerlin, Patrick A. (1993) 'La Communauté, la France, et l'Uruguay Round,' *Commentaire*, no. 63, Autumn.

Migué, Jean-Luc (1993) *Federalism and Free Trade*, Hobart Paper 122, London: Institute of Economic Affairs.

National Consumer Council. (n.d.) *International Trade and the Consumer: Consumer Electronics and the EC's Anti-dumping Policy*, Working Paper 1, London.

National Consumer Council (1993) *International Trade: the Consumer Agenda*, London.

Nunnenkamp, Peter (1993) 'The World Trading System at the Crossroads: Multilateral Trade Negotiations in the Era of Regionalism', *Aussenwirtschaft*, 48, pp.177-201.

OECD Secretariat (1993a) *Assessing the Effects of the Uruguay Round*, Trade Policy Issues 2, Paris.

OECD Secretariat. (1993b) *Economic Outlook*, December 54, Paris.

Olson, Mancur (1982) *The Rise and Decline of Nations: Economic Growth, Stagflation and Social Rigidities*. New Haven and London: Yale University Press.

Sapir, André (1992) 'Regional Integration in Europe', *The Economic Journal*, vol. 102, November, pp.1491-1506.

Schmieding, Holger (1993) *Europe after Maastricht*, Occasional Paper 91, London: Institute of Economic Affairs.

Sinclair, P. J. N. (1993) 'World Trade, Protectionist Follies, and Europe's Options for the Future', *Oxford Review of Economic Policy*, vol. 9, no.3, pp.114-25.

Smith, Adam (1776; ed. Edwin Cannan 1961) *An Inquiry Into the Nature and Causes of the Wealth of Nations*, book IV, chapter II, London: Methuen, University Paperbacks.

Stoeckel, Andrew, David Pearce and Gary Banks (1990). *Western Trade Blocs: Game, Set or Match for Asia-Pacific and the World Economy?* Canberra: Centre for International Economics.

Stopford, John M. (1993) 'European multinationals' competitiveness: Implications for trade policy', in David G. Mayes (ed.) (1993) *The External Implications of European Integration*, New York: Harvester Wheatsheaf.

Tumlir, Jan (1983) 'Strong and Weak Elements in the Concept of European Integration', in Fritz Machlup, Gerhard Fels and Hubertus Müller-Groeling (eds), *Reflections on a Troubled World Economy: Essays in Honour of Herbert Giersch*, London: Macmillan, for the Trade Policy Research Centre.

Winters, L. Alan (1993) 'Expanding EC membership and association accords: recent experience and future prospects', in Kym Anderson and Richard Blackhurst (eds), *Regional Integration in the Global Trading System*, New York: Harvester Wheatsheaf.

Wolf, Martin (1989) 'Why Voluntary Export Restraints: An Historical Analysis', *The World Economy*, vol. 12, no. 3, September, pp.273-92.

Wood, Adrian (1991) 'The Factor Content of North-South Trade in Manufactures Reconsidered', *Weltwirtschaftliches Archiv*, vol. 127, no.4, pp.719-43.

Wood, Adrian (1994) *North-South Trade, Employment and Inequality*, Oxford: Clarendon Press.

World Bank (1992; and other years) *World Development Report: Development and the Environment*, Washington D.C.: Oxford University Press.

World Bank (1993a) *World Development Report: Investing in Health*, Washington D.C.: Oxford University Press.

World Bank (1993b) *Global Economic Prospects and the Developing Countries*, Washington D.C.: Oxford University Press.

C.P.S.
Trade Policy Unit